HOW TO PRODUCE

QUALITY PAINT

Practical guide for a quality paint production

An amazing simplified methods of production

GREAT NELSON

TABLE OF CONTENTS

Chemicals and uses in paint

Chemicals for the production of latex (water based) paint

Chemicals for the production of oil based (Gloss) paint

Chapter Three

Colorant

Color and forms

Color combinations

Chapter Four

Practical methods of production

Production of Emulsion paint (standard quality)

Production of 20 liters of white Egg shell matte paint

Production of 20 liters of white textured matte paint

Production of 20 liters of white flex coat paint

Production of 20 liters of white flexure paint

Production of 20 liters of white Bass coat paint

Production of 20 liters of marble trowel paint

Production of 40 liters of P.O.P Emulsion (standard quality)

Production of 20 liters of white Graffitex paint

Production of 20 liters of white undercoat paint

Production of 20 liters of white marble effect

Production of 20 liters of Dark Anti-rust paint

Production of 20 liters of white Satin paint

Production of 20 liters of Glossy/Oil paint

Production of 20 liters of white text coat paint

Chapter Five

Why start a paint manufacturing firm?

Precautions

Conclusion

CHAPTER ONE

PAINT

Paint is mainly a coating or covering material applied on metallic or non-metallic surfaces for protective or decorative purposes.

BACKGROUND

Paint is a general name for a variety of substances that are made up of a pigment suspended in a liquid or paste medium such as oil or water. Paint is applied in a thin layer to various surfaces such as wood, metal, or stone using a brush, roller, or spray gun. Although its primary function is to preserve the surface on which it is applied, paint also serves as a decorative medium.

Caves in France and Spain include samples of the first known paintings, which were created between 20,000 and 25,000 years ago. Primitive paintings mostly depicted humans and animals, although schematics have also been discovered. Natural soil pigments, charcoal, berry juice, lard, and other readily available natural material were used by early painters to manufacture paint. Blood, as well as milkweed sap. Later, the ancient Chinese, Egyptians, Hebrews, Greeks, and Romans employed more complex materials to make paints for restricted adornment, such as wall painting. Varnishes were made from oils, and pigments including yellow and red ochres, chalk, arsenic sulfide yellow, and malachite green were combined with binders such gum Arabic, lime, egg albumen, and beeswax.

The Egyptians and Hebrews were the first to utilize paint as a protective covering, applying pitches and balsams to the exposed wood of their ships. Some inland wood got protective coats of paint throughout the Middle Ages, although due to paint scarcity, this technique was largely confined to storefronts and signs. Simultaneously, painters began to boil resin with Blood, as well as milkweed sap. Later, the ancient Chinese and Egyptians used oil to make highly miscible (mixable) paints, and fifteenth-century painters were the first to add drying oils to paint, hastening evaporation. They also embraced a new solvent, linseed oil, which remained the most often used solvent until it was superseded by synthetics in the twentieth century.

CLASSIFICATION OF PAINT

Paints are classified base on solvent/medium used in their production.

Latex (water based) Paint - In latex paint, water is the solvent. This is called emulsion paint too.

Gloss (oil based) Paint - In gloss paint, oil is the solvent. The Solvent can be one of petroleum, kerosene, thinner, mineral spirits and so on.

TYPES OF PAINT

There are two types of paints

Decorative Paints.

Industrial Paints

I. **Decorative Paints** are used for interior and exterior house painting. Industrial paints are used for industrial paintings.

Decorative paints include; emulsion, gloss, silk/satin and more while industrial paints include auto paints, marine paints, wood paints, road markings, bright aluminum, bituminous and more.

II. **Industrial Paints** on the other hand are specialized paints which are used predominantly for industrial strength protection and less so, for aesthetic purposes. Also, known as commercial paints.

They include high performance coatings, automotive paints, marine paints, coatings and generic industrial usage paints. In application, such paints are used on steel, glass, iron, aluminum, composite materials, plastic and even wood. These materials make up the body of transformers, machineries, containers, equipment, industrial furniture, pipes and nuts and bolts.

The automobile industry uses industrial paints for painting the body of vehicles which is a large painted surface.

COMPONENTS OF PAINT

Paint is made up of pigments, solvents, binders(resins), and additives.

1. **Pigments** - The pigments give your paint color and not just that, they also give paint agility, opacity (that is, hide the substrate surface) and capacity to cover.

Note. Fillers and extenders are also referred to pigments.

2. **Solvents** - Solvents are water and any other solvents (petroleum, kerosene, thinner etc.)

Used in paint production. Solvent is a medium where the binders, pigments and additives are mixed.

3. **Binders** (Resins) - Binders are constituent that provide a binding, gumming and sticking effect that holds the pigments together to create a dry film on the key constituent that directly pertaining to a paint, performance including surface resistance, washability, adhesion, fade resistance or gloss retention.

4. **Additives** - These are ingredients that provides certain paint properties such as mildew resistance, defoaming, flame retardant, UV stability, good flow and leveling. Simply put additives prevent defects in coating, for example - foam bubbles, sedimentation, poor leveling,

flocculation etc.

CHAPTER TWO

FUNCTIONS OF PAINT

1. Paint is used to protect and extend the life of a surface.

2. It is used to give a high-class finish

3. Paint is used to make a surface attractive

4. It is used to give surfaces loving design and appearance

5. It protects various surfaces from corrosion

6. Paints are used to protect surfaces from negative atmospheric conditions.

7. To promote the clearing process of surfaces

8. To prevent wooden articles from

decomposition, rottenness and many other types of defects.

CLASSIFICATION OF PAINT BASED ON USAGE

1. **Priming**

2. **Undercoating**

3. **Finishing parts.**

1. **Priming Paints** are used to prepare walls or materials before applying finishing paint. Priming ensures better adhesion of paint to the surface, increases paint durability and provides additional protection for the material being painted.

2. **Undercoating paints** are used to prepare

walls or materials before applying finishing paint. Although both priming and undercoating paints serves quite different functions. Primer's act as a foundation for your paint to stick to the wall, undercoat creates a flat and level base for too coats. One easy way to remember is, if a surface is painted use an undercoat, if the surface is new, use a primer. Note. Always use primer/undercoat paints on wall surfaces before painting especially if the wall/surface is porous. The surface is porous when it absorbs water, moisture, oil, odors or stains.

3. **Finishing paints** - This is the final coat of paint applied to a wall or surface.

TOOLS AND MACHINES USED IN PAINT FORMULATION AND PRODUCTION

Mixing drum.

mixing stick.

measuring scale.

digital scale.

electric industrial handheld paint mixer/paint mixing machine.

measuring cup.

Protective wears for paint production.

Industrial hand glove.

Industrial nose mask.

Rubber boot

Thick overall cloth

Rubber Mallet

Plastic bucket / Tin bucket

CHEMICALS AND USES IN PAINT

1. **Water** – It serves as solvent in water-based paint.

2. **Kerosene** – It serve as solvent in oil-based paint

3. **Genipor** – It serves as dispersant.

4. **Calcium carbonate** – This forms the body of the paint.

5. **Titanium dioxide** – It is used for coverage

and colorant.

6. **Biocide, acticide, fungicide, formalin** and **ammonia** – It is used as preservatives.

7. **Defoamer** – This is used to remove foam in paint.

8. **PVA** – This is the gum or binder used in water-based paint.

9. **Alkyd** – This is the gum or binder used in oil-based paint.

10. **Natrosol**, **Bama cork** – This is used as thickener in paint.

11. **Hydrosol** – It is a shining agent in paint.

12. **Kaolin** – It forms the body of paint.

13. **Aluminum silicate** – It is used as a whitening agent in paint.

14. **Marble dust** – It gives rough or sand like texture in water-based paint

15. **Texanol** – It is a shinning agent in paint

16. **Acticide EPW** – Preservative.

17. **Calgon** – It serves as a plasticizer.

18. **Caustic soda** – It serves as a Plasticizer.

19. **Sodium benzoate** – Buffer.

PAINT PRODUCTION TOOLS

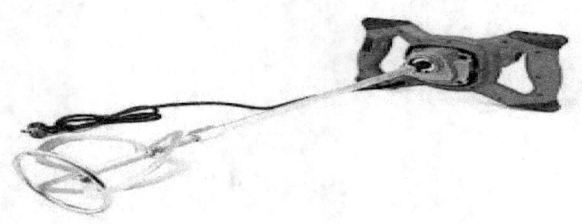

HAND HELD ELECTRIC MIXER

RUBBER MALLET

PLASTIC BUCKETS

BUCKET SEALER

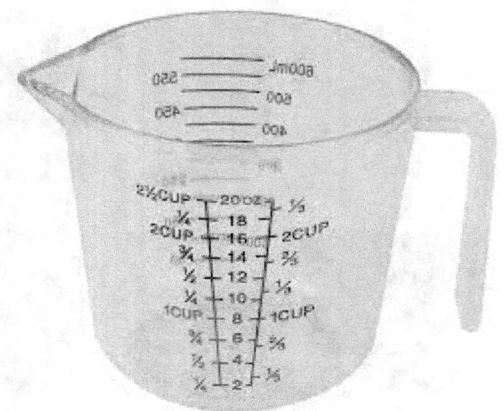

MEASURING CUP

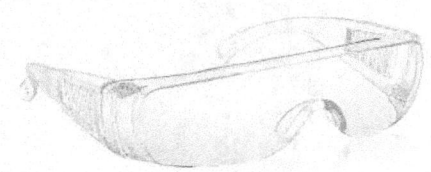

GLASSWEAR

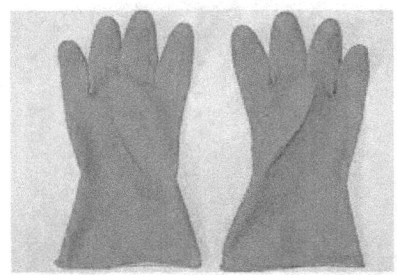

HAND GLOVE

WEIGHING SCALE

PAINT MIXER

NOSE MASK

PAINT PRODUCTION CHEMICALS

ALUMINIUM SILICATE

NATROSOL

GENIPOR

DEFOAMER

KAOLIN

COLOR IRON OXIDE

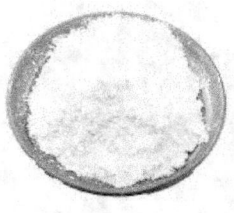

TITANIUM DIOXIDE

WATER THICKENER

AMMONIA   ANTI-SKIN

CALCIUM CARBONATE

CALGON

ALKYD

PVA

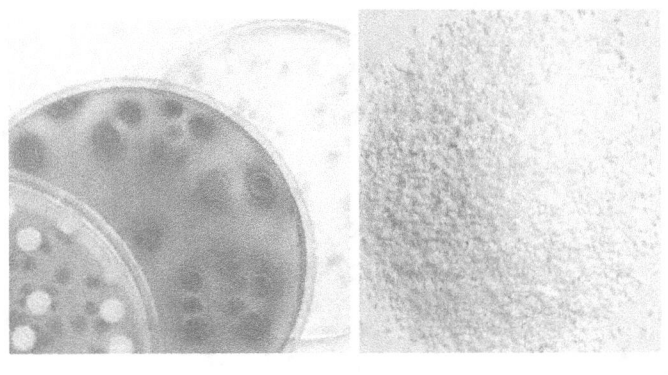

BIOCIDE   MARBLE DUST

FORMALIN

TEXANOL

SODIUM BENZOATE

SOYA LECITHIN

COLOR PASTE

CHEMICALS FOR THE PRODUCTION OF LATEX (WATER BASED) PAINT

1. Genipor

2. Calcium carbonate

3. Titanium dioxide

4. Biocide, acticide, fungicide etc.

5. Defoamer

6. PVA

7. Natrosol, Bama cork

8. Hydrosol

9. Kaolin

10. Aluminum silicate

11. Marble dust

12. Texanol

13. Acticide EPW

14. Calgon

15. Caustic soda.

CHEMICALS FOR THE PRODUCTION OF OIL BASED(GLOSSY) PAINTS

1. **Solvents** - these can be petroleum, thinner, kerosene, toluene, mineral spirit.

2. **Binder (resin)** – alkyd (resins)

3. **Anti-skinning agent** - In oil-based paint production, an anti-skinning agent is usually added to prevent undesirable drying of paint in the paint can. This chemical prevents the paint from caking

or having layer on the surface. The anti-skinning agent prevents the formation of skin in the paint. Methyl Ethyl ketoxime (MEKO) is the most used anti-skinning agent in paints.

4. **Soya lecithin(emulsifier)** - This is one it the

most important chemical in oil-based paints production. Soya lecithin is used as a dispersant suspending agent, an emulsifier, a stabilizer as well as an anti-splatter additive. It has the ability to reduce viscosity and also has anti-settling properties.

5. **Easy Gel** - This is mainly used in oil-based paint production. It is the thickener in oil-based paint. It is rarely used in oil-based paint because the binder (resin) has the ability to thicken the paint too.

6. **Mixed drier** - Mixed drier is one of the main important ingredients of oil-based paint. It accelerates the drying of resin thereby decreasing the drying time of the paint or coating. Mixed drier works as stimulant to boost

the oxidation of the oil and to accelerate the cross- linking process in which oil particles join together.

PAINT PRODUCTION FACTORY

CHAPTER THREE

COLORANT

Color mixing or tinting is one key area producers must be very skilled at. Paints are produced in different colors using colorants that are either in powder form (color oxide) or in paste.

Both color oxide and paste come in primary colors mainly red, blue, green, yellow and black. And most paints colors that we come in secondary colors, to get any color, you want to produce apart from white/brilliant white, all you have to do is to measure the quantity that you need either in oxide or paste and add it to the paint and mix the paint very well.

Other colors also come in tertiary colors in this case, you need to mix 3 or more colors to achieve the color shade. As a paint producer, you must learn how to mix 2-4 different colors to achieve just one color.

The Color Rule

Color rule is the rule such that whenever you are producing paint colors that requires oxide, they are poured inside mixing tank immediately after proper mixing of titanium dioxide but if it is in paste form it come last. This is because paste blend easily with paints than oxide. Oxide required timely and proper mixing to blend with the paint.

Pigment

Titanium dioxide

Rubine red

Chrome red

Carbon black

Yellow chrome

Chrome oxide

Halogen green

Phthalocyanine

Lemon chrome

Zinc chromate

Brown umber

Prussian

Zinc oxide

Molybdate oxide

Red Scholz

Yellow Scholz

COLOR AND FORMS

Paste - liquid

Green paste - liquid paste

Black paste - liquid paste

Orange paste - liquid paste

Blue paste - liquid paste

Red paste - liquid paste

Yellow paste – liquid paste

Oxide – powder

Green oxide

Blue chrome oxide

Red oxide

Yellow oxide

Carbon black oxide

Red Scholz oxide

Yellow chrome oxide

Green chrome oxide

The knowledge of color combination is very important in paint production; it is divided into

iii. Primary color

ii. Secondary color

iii. Tertiary color

Primary colors; these are the basic colors which are

Red,

Blue,

Yellow.

Secondary colors

These are the combination of two or more primary color. They are

Blue + yellow = green

Red + yellow = orange

Red + blue = purple

Yellow + white = cream

Blue + white = sky blue

White + black = grey

Little red + Bluer = lilac

Yellow + black = beige

Red + black = brown

Red + yellow + black = brown

Tertiary colors

These are the combination of two or more secondary colors or combination of secondary color and primary color, example

Green + yellow = lemon

Green + red = brown

Orange + blue = brown

Cream + little black = brown

COLOR COMBINATIONS

White color

Brilliant white – 2-8kg of titanium dioxide, 1-2kg of aluminum silicate

Off white – 50-100g of yellow oxide after titanium dioxide

Cream color

Cream 3040 – 250g of yellow oxide after titanium dioxide

Banana 4052 – 100-120g of yellow paste at the end of production

Sun flower – 600g of yellow oxide after titanium dioxide

Grey color

Ice grey 8087 – 50g of blue paste, 2 teaspoons of black paste

Silver grey 9093 – 70g of blue paste, 1 teaspoon of black paste

Blue color

Light blue – 2 spoons of blue paste at the end of production.

Aquamarine – 50g of blue paste, 4 spoon of yellow paste.

Sky blue – 4 spoons of blue paste, 1 spoon of yellow paste.

Green color

Leaf green – 200g of yellow paste, 30-40g of blue paste.

Light green – 100g of yellow paste, 15g of blue paste

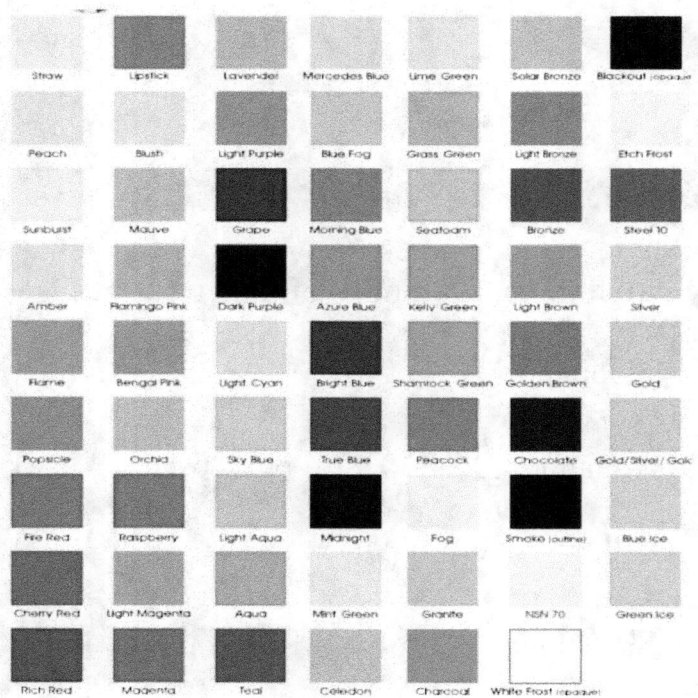

COLOR CHART

CHAPTER FOUR

PRACTICAL METHODS OF PRODUCTION

PRODUCTION OF EMULSION (STANDARD QUALITY)

Materials needed for 20litres

1. Clean Water (room temperature)

2. Titanium dioxide

3. Calcium carbonate

4. Aluminum silicate

5. Genipor

6. Defoamer

7. Formalin

8. PVA/Acrylic

9. Natrosol

10. Calgon

11. 1 bucket

WHITE EMULSION PAINT FORMULATION (STANDARD QUALITY)

Materials needed

1. Clean Water (room temperature) - 8litres

2. Calcium carbonate - 12kg

3. Aluminum silicate - 100g

4. Genipor - 50g

5. Titanium dioxide - 100g

6. Defoamer - 50g

7. PVA/ Acrylic - 1.2kg

8. Natrosol - 85g

9. Paste - NA

10. Oxide - NA

Procedure

Get all your materials to be used ready.

1. Pour 6litres of water into the mixing drum or mixer.

2. Pour your measured titanium dioxide into the mixing drum, mix very well for 10minutes. Note. Titanium dioxide is the first chemical to pour into mixing drum.

3. Add color to the mixer, if the paint requires color, you add.

4. Pour calcium carbonate, stir for 10-15 minutes.

5. Pour Aluminum silicate.

6. Pour Genipor and stir.

7. Add defoamer.

8. Pour formalin, stir for 5minutes.

9. Pour PVA/ Acrylic, mix properly.

10. Add color paste if necessary.

11. Mix natrosol in a liter of water and pour, then stir for 5-10minutes.

12. Pour Calgon and mix.

13. Package.

PRODUCTION OF 20LITRES OF WHITE EGG SHELL MATTE

Materials needed

1. Clean Water (room temperature) - 6 liters

2. Titanium dioxide - 3kg

3. Calcium carbonate - 4kg

4. PVA(Acrylic) - 10kg

5. Genipor - 50g

6. Acticide - 100g

7. Sodium benzoate - 100g

8. Natrosol - 100g

9. Texanol - 100g

Procedure

1. Pour 5litres of water into the mixing drum.

2. Add genipor and stir very well.

3. Add titanium dioxide and mix.

4. Add color (if necessary) and stir.

5. Add calcium carbonate, stir very well to dissolve the lumps.

6. Add Acrylic, stir.

7. In a separate bowl mix 100g of natrosol in 1kg or 1litre of water and add to the paint.

8. Add buffer acticide and texanol and stir.

9. Package, your eggshell matte is ready.

PRODUCTION OF TEXTURED MATTE PAINT (COLOR- WHITE, 20LITRES)

Materials needed

1. Clean Water (room temperature) - 8litres

2. Titanium dioxide - 2kg

3. Calcium carbonate - 12kg

4. PVA(Acrylic) - 4kg

5. Smooth marble dust - 2kg

6. Genipor - 50g

7. Defoamer - 50g

8. Acticide - 100g

9. Sodium Benzoate - 70g

10. Natrosol - 120g

11. Kaolin - 2kg

12. Caustic soda - N/A

13. Paste - N/A

14. Oxide - N/A

Procedure

1. Pour 7litres of water into your mixing drum.

2. Add titanium dioxide and stir very well.

3. Add calcium carbonate and stir.

4. Add kaolin and stir very well.

5. Add color (if necessary).

6. Pour the smooth marble dust and stir very well.

7. Pour Genipor and stir.

8. Add defoamer and stir.

9. Pour in PVA/Acrylic.

10. Mix natrosol in a separate bowl with 1litre of water and pour into the mixing drum.

11. Add buffer and acticide, stir very well.

12. Package.

PRODUCTION OF 20LITRES OF WHITE FLEX COAT PAINT

Materials needed

1. Clean Water (room temperature) - 8litres

2. Titanium dioxide - 1kg

3. Calcium carbonate - 24kg

4. PVA(Acrylic) - 4kg

5. Genipor - 50g

6. Acticide - 100g

7. Sodium benzoate - 100g

8. Natrosol - 100g

9. Paste - N/A

10. Oxide - N/A

Procedure

1. Pour 7litres of water into your mixing drum.

2. Pour titanium dioxide and stir very well.

3. Add your color (if necessary) and stir.

4. Add calcium carbonate and keep stirring.

5. Pour in Genipor and keep stirring.

6. Pour in PVA/Acrylic and stir.

7. Mix natrosol in 1litre of water and pour into

the mixing drum.

8. Pour in sodium benzoate and acticide, stir very well for 10minutes.

9. Package.

PRODUCTION OF 20LITRES OF WHITE FLEXTURED PAINT

Materials needed

1. Clean Water (room temperature) - 8litres

2. Titanium dioxide - 2kg

3. Calcium carbonate - 12kg

4. Smooth marble dust - 12kg

5. Genipor - 100g

6. Defoamer - 100g

7. Acticide - 100g

8. Natrosol - 125g

9. PVA/Acrylic - 3kg

10. Paste - N/A

11. Oxide - N/A

Procedure

1. Pour 7litres of water into the drum.

2. Add titanium dioxide and stir.

3. Add calcium carbonate and keep stirring.

4. Add color (if necessary).

5. Add smooth marble dust and stir well.

6. Pour Genipor and Stir very well.

7. Pour in PVA/Acrylic and stir very well.

8. Pour defoamer and stir.

9. Mix natrosol in 1litre of water in a separate bowl and add, then stir very well.

10. Add acticide and stir very well for 10-15minutes.

11. Package.

PRODUCTION OF 20LITRES OF WHITE BASE COAT PAINT

Materials needed

Clean Water (room temperature) - 6litres

Titanium dioxide - N/A

Calcium carbonate - 24kg

Kaolin - N/A

Aluminum silicate - N/A

Genipor - 50g

Acticide - 100g

PVA/Acrylic - 4kg

Natrosol - 100g

Sodium benzoate - 100g

Paste - N/A

Oxide - N/A

Procedure

1. Pour 5litres of water into your drum.

2. Add calcium carbonate and stir.

3. Pour in your Genipor and stir.

4. Pour in your PVA /Acrylic and mix well.

5. Mix natrosol in 1litre of water and pour into the mixing drum.

6. Pour in sodium benzoate and acticide and stir well for 10minutes.

7. Package.

PRODUCTION OF 20LITRES OF MARBLE TROWEL PAINT

Materials needed

1. Clean Water (room temperature) – 6 liters

2. Titanium dioxide - N/A

3. Calcium carbonate - N/A

4. PVA/Acrylic - 4kg

5. Rough marble dust - 24kg (you are to buy

three different colors of rough marble dust, 8kg each color).

6. Genipor - 50g

7. Defoamer - 50g

8. Natrosol - 150g

9. Calgon - N/A

10. Sodium benzoate - 50g

11. Paste - N/A

12. Oxide - N/A

Procedure

1. Pour 5litres of water into the drum.

2. Add your rough marble dust and mix very

well.

3. Pour PVA/Acrylic and stir well.

4. Pour in your Genipor and stir very well.

5. Mix natrosol with 1litre of water and pour into the mixing drum.

6. Pour sodium benzoate and stir.

7. Pour acticide and stir very well for 10minutes.

8. Package.

PRODUCTION OF 40LITRES OF VANISH PAINT (COLOR N/A)

Materials needed

1. Drier - 1kg

2. Kerosene - 4litres

3. Light resin - 34kg

Note. If you are producing a 20litres drum, divide by 2

Procedure

1. Pour in your kerosene into mixing drum.

2. Pour in your light resin.

3. Add drier.

PRODUCTION OF 20LITRES OF P.O.P EMULSION PAINT (STANDARD QUALITY)

Materials needed

1. Clean Water (room temperature) - 8litres

2. Titanium dioxide - 2kg

3. Calcium carbonate - 10kg

4. Kaolin - N/A

5. Aluminum silicate - 1.5kg

6. Genipor - 150g

7. Defoamer - 150g

8. Acticide - 150g

9. PVA/Acrylic - 3kg

10. Natrosol - 200g

11. Calgon - 40g

Procedure

1. Pour 7litres of water into the drum.

2. Pour titanium dioxide and stir very well.

3. Pour calcium carbonate and stir until smooth.

4. Pour Aluminum silicate and stir well.

5. Pour Genipor and stir well.

6. Add defoamer.

7. Mix natrosol with 1litre if water in a separate bowl and pour into the mixing drum.

8. Add Calgon and stir well.

9. Pour PVA (Acrylic).

10. Add acticide and mix very well.

11. Package.

PRODUCTION OF 20LITRES WHITE OF GRAFFITEX PAINT

Materials needed

1.Clean Water - 8litres

2. Titanium dioxide - 1kg

3. Calcium carbonate - 5kg

4. PVA/Acrylic - 5kg

5. Genipole - 50g

6. Acticide - 100g

7. Sodium benzoate - 100g

8. Natrosol - 120g

9. A1 stone - 1kg

10. Smooth marble dust - 25kg

Procedure

1. Pour 7litres of water.

2. Add titanium dioxide, mix well.

3. Pour in color If necessary.

4. Pour Genipole, stir very well.

5. Pour calcium carbonate.

6. Pour smooth marble, stir very well.

7. Pour A1 stone and stir.

8. Pour PVA(Acrylic), stir very well.

9. Mix natrosol in 1litre of water and pour into the mixing drum.

10. Pour acticide and buffer, stir very well for

10minutes.

11. Package.

PRODUCTION OF 20 LITERS OF WHITE UNDERCOAT PAINT

Materials needed

1. Kerosene - 5litres

2. Titanium dioxide - 5kg

3. Calcium carbonate - 10kg

4. Mixed drier - 500g

5. Alkyd resin - 10kg

6. Soya lecithin (optional) - 100g

7. Anti -skin(optional) - 100g

Procedure

1. Pour alkyd resin into your mixing drum.

2. Mix titanium dioxide in 1litre of kerosene, make sure its smooth before pouring into mixing drum.

3. Pour in kerosene and stir well.

4. Pour in calcium carbonate and stir well.

5. Pour anti-skin (meke) and stir (it is optional).

6. Pour in soya lecithin and stir (it is optional).

7. Pour your drier and stir very simple.

8. Package.

PRODUCTION OF 20LITRES OF WHITE MARBLE EFFECT PAINT

Materials needed

1. Water - 8litres

2. Titanium dioxide - 1kg

3. Calcium carbonate - 25kg

4. PVA(Acrylic) - 6kg

5. Genipole - 50g

6. Acticide - 100g

7. Sodium benzoate - 100g

8. Natrosol - 100g

Procedure

1. Pour 7litres of water.

2. Pour titanium dioxide and mix well.

3. Add your color if necessary.

4. Pour calcium carbonate and stir very well.

5. Pour Genipole and stir well.

6. Add PVA/Acrylic and stir continuously.

7. Mix natrosol in 1litre of water and pour into the drum.

8. Add sodium benzoate and stir.

9. Pour Acticide and stir well.

10. Package.

PRODUCTION OF 20 LITERS OF DARK RED ANTI RUST PAINT

Material needed

1. Kerosene - 10litres

2. Talc - 2kg

3. Calcium carbonate - 2kg

4. Mixed drier - 350g

5. Alkyd resin - 7kg

6. Soya lecithin (optional) - 350g

7. Anti-skin (optional) - 350g

8. Aluminum silicate - 1kg

9. Barite or clay - 1kg

10. Red oxide - 2kg

11. Carbon black oxide - 1kg

Procedure

1. Pour 5litres of kerosene into the mixing drum, balance of the kerosene will be added as you continue production.

2. Pour alkyd resin and stir on.

3. Pour in your aluminum silicate and stir well.

4. Pour in your talc and stir on.

5. Pour calcium carbonate and mix very well.

6. Pour barite and stir very simple.

7. Pour your oxide (red and black) and stir well.

8. Pour soya lecithin and mix well.

9. Pour anti-skin and stir very well.

10.Pour mixed drier and stir very vigorously

until a perfect mix is   achieved.

11. Package

PRODUCTION OF 20 LITERS OF WHITE SATIN PAINT.

Materials needed

1. Water - 8litres

2. Titanium dioxide - 6.5kg

3. Acticide EPW - 40g

4. PVA(Acrylic) - 12kg

5. Aluminum silicate - 2kg

6. Genipole - 80g

7. Defoamer - 150g

8. Acticide - 250g

9. Sodium benzoate - 400g

10. Natrosol - 60g

11. Calgon - 150g

12. Texanol - 800g

Procedure

1. Pour 7litres of water into the drum.

2. Pour titanium dioxide, mix very well to mix perfectly.

3. Add your color if necessary.

4. Pour Calgon and stir very well.

5. Pour Genipole and stir well.

6. Pour defoamer.

7. Pour Acticide and stir.

8. Add acticide EPW and keep stirring.

9. Pour sodium benzoate and stir very well.

10. Pour PVA(Acrylic) and stir.

11. Pour natrosol and stir well.

12. Pour your color paste if necessary.

13. Pour texanol and stir very vigorously until a perfect mix.

14. Package.

PRODUCTION OF 20 LITRES OF GLOSSY / OIL PAINT

Materials needed

1. Kerosene -- 10litres

2. Titanium dioxide -- 2.5kg

3. Calcium carbonate -- 5kg

4. Mixed drier -- 300g

5. Alkyd resin -- 10kg

6. Easy Gel (optional) -- 50g

7. Soya lecithin -- 50g

8. Anti-skin -- 50g

Procedure

1. Pour kerosene into the drum.

2. Pour alkyd resin and stir well.

3. Pour titanium dioxide and stir well.

4. Add calcium carbonate and stir well.

5. Add easy gel, stir well.

6. Pour color oxide if necessary.

7. Pour mixed drier and stir well.

8. Pour color paste, if necessary, stir well for 10minutes.

9. Package.

PRODUCTION OF 20LITRES OF WHITE TEXT COAT PAINT

Materials needed

1. Water - 6litres

2. Titanium dioxide - 600g

3. Calcium carbonate - 12 - 13kg

4. Aluminum silicate - 300g

5. Marble dust - 7kg

6. Genipole - 150g

7. PVA(Acrylic) - 1.7 - 1.8kg

8. Defoamer - 150g

9. Natrosol - 150g

10. Acticide -30g

11. Calgon - 50g

Procedure

1. Pour 5litres of water into mixing drum.

2. Pour titanium dioxide and stir well.

3. Add color oxide if necessary.

4. Pour calcium carbonate and stir well.

5. Add aluminum silicate and mix well.

6. Pour Genipole.

7. Pour defoamer and stir well.

8. Pour acticide and stir well.

9. Pour PVA/Acrylic and stir well.

10. Pour marble dust and stir aggressively.

11. Add color paste if necessary.

12. Pour natrosol and mix well.

13. Pour Calgon and stir very well.

14. Package.

CHAPTER FIVE

WHY START A PAINT MANUFACTURING FIRM?

PAINT FIRM

1. There is free entry and exit due to the friendly capital required to set up a paint making business.

2. Operating costs are relatively low

3. New entrants get attracted to the paint making business due to primarily the inefficiency in regulatory practices by government agencies.

4. There are 3 tiers in paint manufacturing industry, you can choose to belong to any tier base on your capacity.

5. By becoming a manufacturer of paint, you become a participant in building construction industry value chain.

6. Low setup capital requirement

7. It is highly lucrative.

8. The raw materials are easy to access.

9. Expired paint products can be recycled into new product thereby reducing losses.

PRECAUTIONS

Always ensure that your eyes, nose and hands are covered with protective wears during paint production.

Ensure that there is enough ventilation in the factory to avoid choking.

Do not eat during paint production to avoid being poisoned by the chemical used for production.

Ensure you wash your hands thoroughly with running water after paint production.

Ensure that natrosol is dissolved in a clean room temperature water before pouring into your paint mixture.

Ammonia solution has a choking smell. Do not put your face directly to the container of ammonia to avoid being choked.

During production, do not pour ammonia into natrosol to avoid explosion which can cause damage on the person's body.

Do not drink paint chemicals, if by mistake

swallowed take enough water and consult your doctor immediately.

Keep all chemicals out of the reach of children.

CONCLUSION

Paint is produced when raw materials such as colorants, extender, binder, thickener, antifoam, pH. adjuster etc. are dissolved in solvent either water or oil. During the process of production, the mixture is homogenously mixed to form paint and during application to the substrate, the water oil which act as the thinner or medium, evaporates leaving behind the film.

The paint and coating manufacturing business is essential and plays a critical function in certain sectors of the economy since it provides protective and enhancing finishes for a variety of items in various end-use industries. Paints and varnishes *are* used to conceal a wide range of items.

www.ingramcontent.com/pod-product-compliance
Lightning Source LLC
Chambersburg PA
CBHW062355290526
45794CB00005B/2233